by Isabel Thomas

What Are Volcanoes?

Volcanoes are peaks. Things escape out of volcanoes from deep underground. These things **erupt** from an opening called a crater.

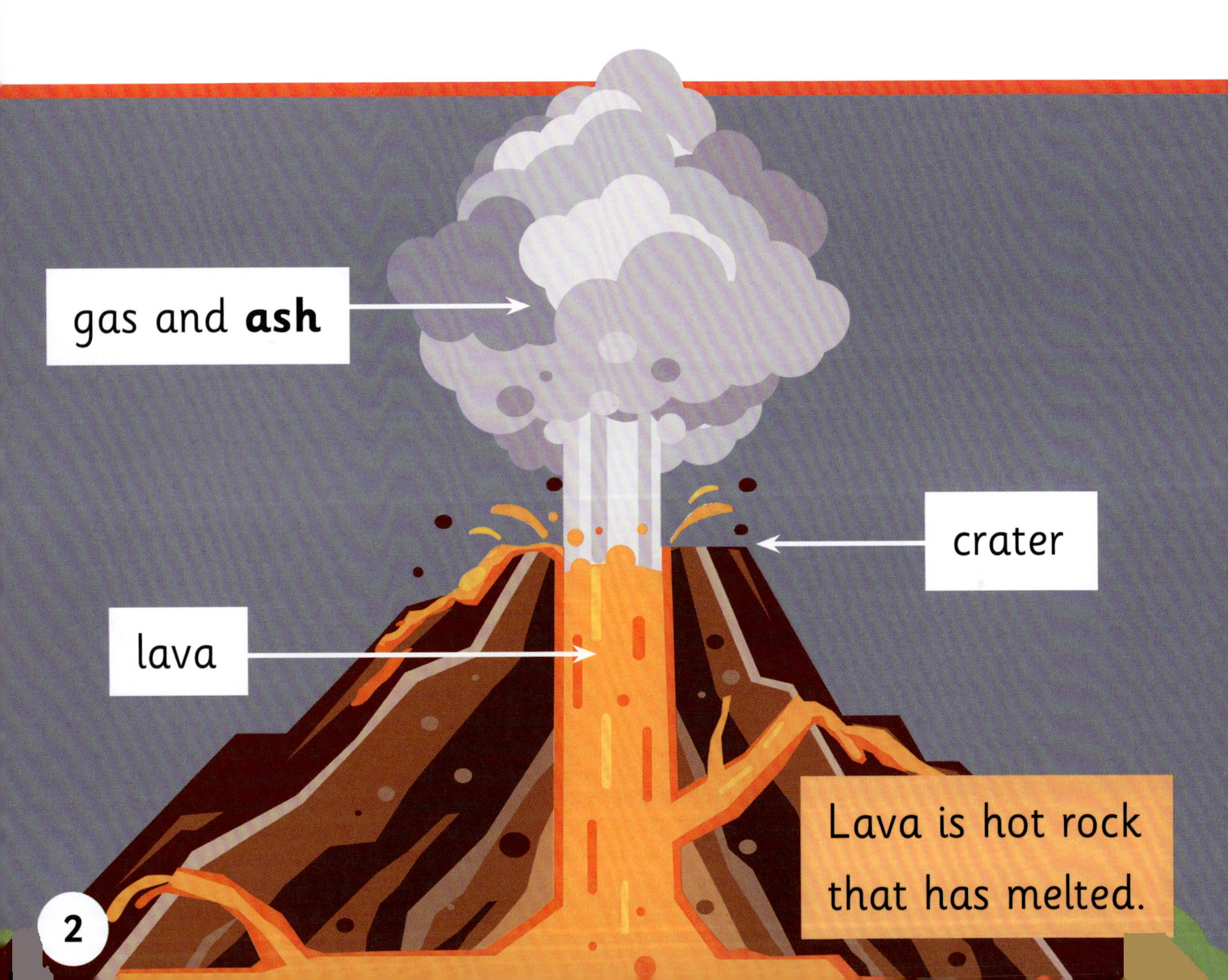

Volcanoes are dangerous places.

- Lava can be five times hotter than an oven!
- Some gases are **toxic**.
- Ash can choke animals.

Which Creatures Live Near Volcanoes?

This is a volcano in Africa. The water in the nearby lake is hot. It is so toxic, it can kill most animals. Look closely. Can you see any animals?

Huge flocks of flamingoes live in the toxic lake! Thick scales stop their legs from burning. They can drink water that is almost boiling.

When this volcano erupted, rivers of lava flowed out. It killed everything in its path.

The hot lava melted roads and cars.

The lava became solid rock again once it had cooled. Lava crickets live on the solid lava. They eat dirt that collects in cracks.

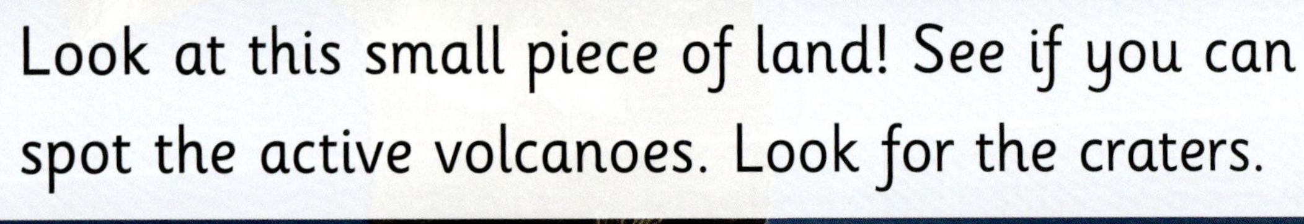

Look at this small piece of land! See if you can spot the active volcanoes. Look for the craters.

One volcano has erupted twice in the last ten years.

Lots of rare animals live here. They survived the eruptions by staying away from the lava. Take a look at some of them.

These lizards live near the coast. However, once a year, they climb into a volcano.

The lizards lay eggs in the ash in the crater.

The ash keeps this lizard's eggs snug and safe.

This volcano is just off the coast of Antarctica. When it erupted, land was covered in toxic smoke and ash.

Many creatures live on the volcanic land.
The volcano eruption covered the birds in ash.
They were dirty, but they still survived.

Underwater Volcanoes

Volcanoes are found underwater, too. When they erupt, lava flows across the sea bed. Then boiling **acid** bubbles out.

Shrimp like to live in the acid water near eruptions. The shrimp's antenna helps it to detect the hottest water. It then avoids this hot spot and stays safe.

This volcano is deep under the sea. The water inside the crater is hot, cloudy and toxic.

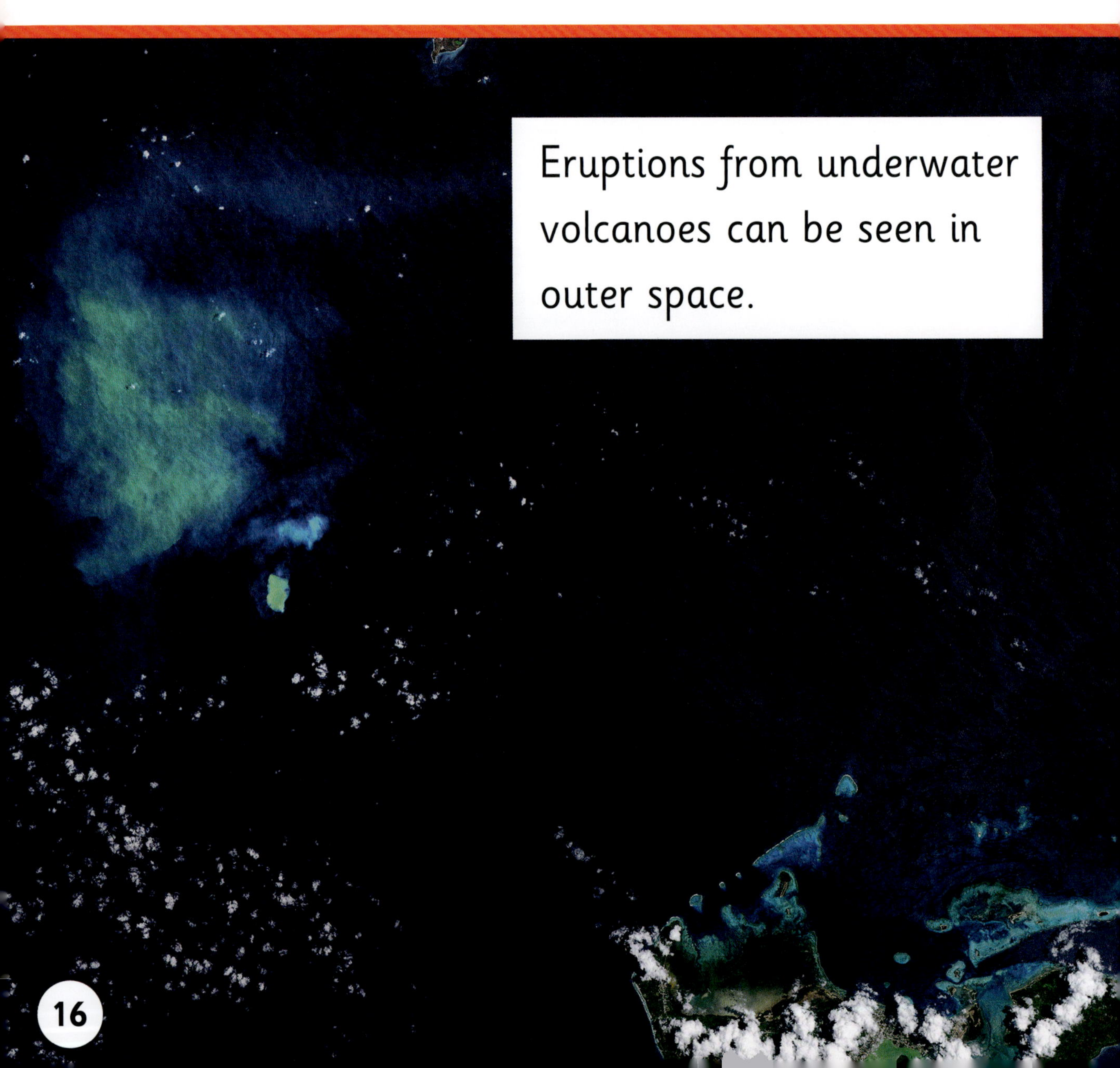

Eruptions from underwater volcanoes can be seen in outer space.

Hammerhead sharks swim near underwater volcanoes.

Some underwater volcanoes attract sharks. An underwater volcano in the Pacific has been nicknamed the 'Sharkcano'.

This underwater volcano has a **cone**. It is as high as a city apartment block. Each time the volcano erupts, the cone grows bigger.

Thousands of different creatures live on the cone. Here are some that have adapted to the toxic water.

crabs

barnacles

limpets

shrimp

Life Around Volcano Craters

Animals are not found near the crater of an active volcano. Toxic gases escape from the volcano.

Plants can be stronger than animals. This active volcano is covered in plants.

Exploring Volcanoes

Volcanoes are dangerous places for humans. However, robots can explore volcanoes safely.

Many creatures live near volcanoes. Robots are helping us to discover new animals.

Spider crabs live near underwater volcanoes.

Glossary

acid: a liquid that can burn many things

ash: the powder left after something has been burned

cone: the top part of a volcano, which includes the crater

erupt: to explode, sending lava bursting out

toxic: poisonous

Index